ROTTERDAM

THE CITY AT A GLANCE

CW00470153

The Red Apple
Kees Christiaanse's elegant st
dominates the north bank of
Maas, and overlooks the bar
See p065

Willemsbrug
Designed by Cornelis Veerling, the distinctive
red 65m pylons of this bridge, opened in 1981,
connect the north bank to Noordereiland.

The Bridge
Unilever's HQ is not a bridge but a skyscraper
lying on its side straddling a margarine
factory. It is supported on 25m-tall stilts.
See p072

Erasmusbrug
UNStudio's dramatic structure has become
a symbol of the city and links the centre
of town to the redeveloping south bank.
See p010

De Rotterdam
Overshadowing Renzo Piano's leaning KPN
Telecom Building, once the centrepiece
on Wilhelminapier, Rem Koolhaas' iconic
'vertical city' is the country's largest edifice.
See p012

Las Palmas
Sharing its renovated warehouse home with
the Nederlands Fotomuseum (T 203 0405)
is Herman den Blijker's cavernous restaurant.
See p052

Montevideo Tower
The Netherlands' tallest residential structure
marks the point from where the huddled
masses once emigrated to the New World.
Otto Reuchlinweg

NEIGHBOURHOODS

THE AREAS YOU NEED TO KNOW AND WHY

To help you navigate the city, we've chosen the most interesting districts (see below and the map inside the back cover) and colour-coded our featured venues, according to their location; those venues that are outside these areas are not coloured.

MUSEUMPARK

Beautifully laid out by architects OMA, the park itself contains Het Nieuwe Instituut (see p076), the Kunsthal (see p078) and grand art collections (see p030). Feeding into it is Witte De Withstraat, a great strip of boutiques, design galleries, cafés and bars such as De Witte Aap (see p036).

LLOYDKWARTIER

Renovation rules in this new 'hood, where the old Lloyd shipping line HQ has been converted into apartments; a one-time electricity substation is now the Stroom hotel (see p022); and the Schiecentrale power station is a TV and recording studio. The most striking building is the Shipping and Transport College (see p034).

OUDE WESTEN

Still a little edgy, Oude Westen is home to boisterous bars, music venues and all-day hangout Rotown (Nieuwe Binnenweg 17-19, T 436 2669). On the same street you'll find Dutch product design, rare vinyl and ethnic emporiums. Nearby is trad eaterie De Pijp (see p048) and to the east is Chinatown.

WATERFRONT/NOORDEREILAND

Noordereiland, the island in the Maas, is an urban 'village' with leafy boulevards and tranquil squares. Waterfront includes Rotterdam's earliest harbour, Oude Haven, which is surrounded by restaurants such as Mooii (see p051), café/bars, and Europe's first skyscraper, the Witte Huis (see p013).

SCHEEPVAARTKWARTIER

Spread about the pretty Shipping Quarter are several buildings and streets that survived the WWII blitz. Come here for fine dining at Parkheuvel (see p047) and the design stores and bars of converted warehouse Westelijk Handelsterrein (Van Vollenhovenstraat 15, T 5175 6281).

CITY CENTRE

Coolsingel, the city's retail hub, is home to the big brands, whereas the independent boutiques cluster around Nieuwemarkt/Pannekoekstraat and Oude Binnenweg. Just north of Hofplein and to the east of Centraal Station (see p074) is Central District East, an emerging zone of clubs, bars and novel shops like Groos (see p082).

DELFSHAVEN

Around the Voorhaven and Achterhaven inlets is a huddle of streets dating back six centuries to when the city of Delft wanted its own harbour, to avoid paying tolls to Rotterdam. The district is now an affluent suburb peppered with antiques shops, sailing boats and local restaurants.

KOP VAN ZUID

The Erasmusbrug (see p010) sparked the redevelopment of the south bank, which boasts towers by Foster + Partners, OMA (see p012), Renzo Piano and Mecanoo. A new footbridge from Hotel New York (see p017) connects to Katendrecht and its dynamic dining square, Deliplein.

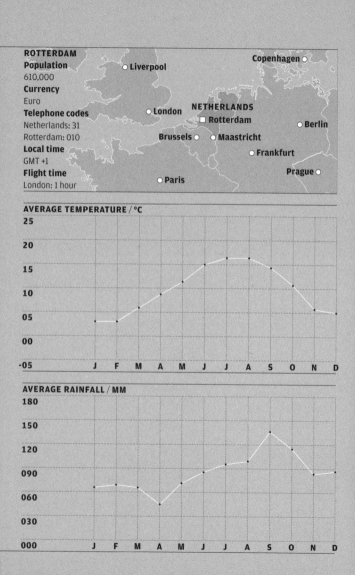

ROTTERDAM
Population
610,000
Currency
Euro
Telephone codes
Netherlands: 31
Rotterdam: 010
Local time
GMT +1
Flight time
London: 1 hour

Liverpool
Copenhagen
London
NETHERLANDS
Rotterdam
Berlin
Brussels
Maastricht
Frankfurt
Prague
Paris

AVERAGE TEMPERATURE / °C

25

20

15

10

05

00

-05

J F M A M J J A S O N D

AVERAGE RAINFALL / MM

180

150

120

090

060

030

000

J F M A M J J A S O N D

ESSENTIAL INFO

FACTS, FIGURES AND USEFUL ADDRESSES

TOURIST OFFICE
Coolsingel 195-197
T 790 0185
www.rotterdam.info

TRANSPORT
Airport transfer to city centre
Bus 33 departs regularly for Centraal Station. The journey takes 20 minutes
Car hire
Europcar
T 437 1826
Public transport
www.ret.nl
Taxis
St Job Taxi
T 425 7000
Cabs can also be hailed on the street
Tourist card
A three-day Rotterdam Welcome Card (€17.50) grants unlimited use of public transport and discounts to attractions

EMERGENCY SERVICES
Emergencies
T 112
24-hour pharmacy
T 020 694 8709
Call for weekly rota

EMBASSIES
British Embassy
Lange Voorhout 10
The Hague
T 070 427 0427
www.gov.uk/government/world/
netherlands
US Embassy
Lange Voorhout 102
The Hague
T 070 310 2209
thehague.usembassy.gov

POSTAL SERVICES
Post office
Easy Repro
William Boothlaan 15a
www.postnl.nl
Shipping
DHL
Kiotoweg 5
T 244 4444

BOOKS
Architectural Guide to Rotterdam
by Paul Groenendijk and Piet Vollaard (010 Publishers)
Dutch Design: A History by Mienke Simon Thomas (Reaktion Books)

WEBSITES
Architecture/Design
www.architectuurinrotterdam.nl
www.hetnieuweinstituut.nl
Newspaper
www.nrc.nl

EVENTS
Art Rotterdam Week
www.artrotterdamweek.com
International Film Festival
www.filmfestivalrotterdam.com

COST OF LIVING
Taxi from Rotterdam The Hague Airport to the city centre
€25
Cappuccino
€2.50
Packet of cigarettes
€6
Daily newspaper
€1.80
Bottle of champagne
€40

INTRODUCTION
THE CHANGING FACE OF THE URBAN SCENE

Contemporary Rotterdam remains very much defined by 14 May 1940, when the centre was levelled by a German bombing raid and subsequent firestorm. The destruction led to an almost entirely 20th-century-built environment, producing a place with a strong commitment to the 'new' in all its forms. For the visitor, this means a Dutch city without historic houses and leafy canals, and a fiercely thrusting skyline drafted by some of the world's great architects, many of whom call Rotterdam home. Recent additions include OMA's colossal De Rotterdam (see p012), luxury hotel Mainport (see p020) and a revamped Centraal Station (see p074).

Many people are also drawn here by the city's cultural approach, a no-nonsense, multicultural ethic (just under 50 per cent of the population is foreign-born) celebrating innovation, inspiration and change. Gentrifying neighbourhoods such as Katendrecht and Central District East are offering young creatives an affordable arena in which to spread their wings, and formerly vacant wharves and warehouses house designers, fashionistas and artists from all over. Then there's the wave of city-centric shopping experiences in slick surroundings, and a local cuisine that ranges from simple, regionally sourced dishes to cutting-edge molecular cooking. Add to this the usual offbeat Dutch approach to life, plus the charm of a European destination relatively untouched by international tourism, and you have a fabulously attractive city.

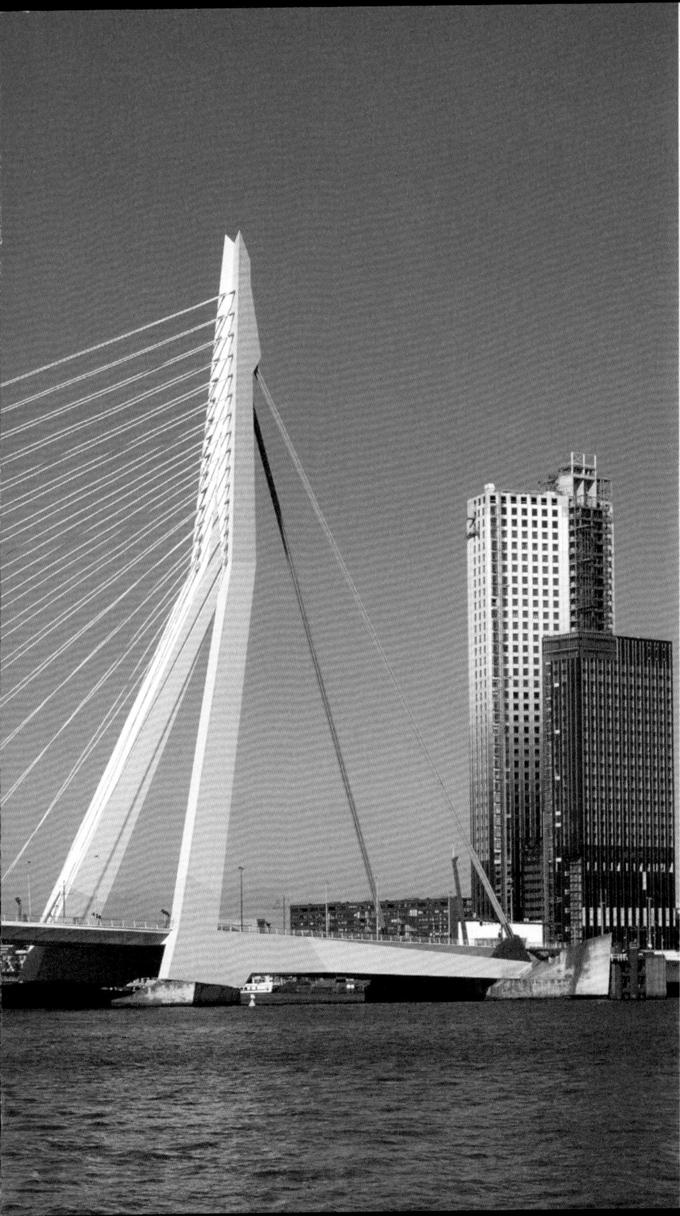

De Rotterdam

Rem Koolhaas' third finished hometown project, after the Kunsthal (see p078) and 1988's Patio Villa in Kralingen-Oost, is as hulking as the architect's reputation. Comprising 160,000 sq m of floor area shared across 7,588 rooms, De Rotterdam is the nation's largest building and fits with the city's 'Manhattan on the Maas' feel. Completed in 2013, it was conceived as a mixed-use vertical city with offices, flats, conference facilities, exhibition space, a hotel (see p016), shops and restaurants. The three 150m-tall interconnected glass towers are best viewed from a car, as the exteriors seem to dance when observed from changing perspectives. It remains to be seen whether the interior – reportedly described by Koolhaas as 'a cheap office building' – is as popular with tenants.
Van der Vormplein 19, www.derotterdam.nl

Witte Huis

At 43m high, the 1898 Witte Huis can lay claim to be the first skyscraper in Europe. Designed by architect Willem Molenbroek, backed by businessmen Gerrit and Herman van der Schuit, the building was inspired by Gerrit's visit to New York. The initial idea was to create a Central Park-style French château, but the traditional New York steel frame was eschewed for load-bearing walls up to 1.4m thick. At the time, the critical appraisal was fairly negative, not least because of the white glazed facade, but it has become popular, partly because of the viewing platform on the roof (now open during events only) and partly because it is one of the few significant prewar buildings left in town. To glimpse the interiors, visit Grand Café Het Witte Huis (T 414 2142) on the ground floor.
Wijnhaven 3/Geldersekade

Schouwburgplein

Although surrounded by cultural venues, this square used to be underwhelming as an urban space. From 1990 to 1996, landscape architect Adriaan Geuze of West 8 reconfigured it as a 'theatre square', raising it 35cm and creating zones with different paving. The four red hydraulic light masts are a typically Rotterdam solution to a lack of historical context: make it modern instead.

HOTELS

WHERE TO STAY AND WHICH ROOMS TO BOOK

Despite being a city full of designers, Rotterdam has only recently started to become a design destination. Owing to its history as a no-nonsense, working city, it hasn't always had the sort of pleasure palaces found in the more frequently visited European hotspots. That said, the available hotels will not disappoint, especially SS Rotterdam (3e Katendrechtsehoofd 25, T 297 3090), a renovated 1950s ocean liner moored in the Maashaven, and the Mainport (see p020). Additionally, there is the 2014 opening of the nHow (Wilhelminakade 137, T 206 7600) in OMA's De Rotterdam (see p012). Styled around an 'architecture and art' motif, the hotel's 278 slick rooms are matched only by its views over the Maas.

Further cutting-edge accommodation is at Stroom (see p022), a converted electricity substation. More ornamented, but equally design-led, is Suitehotel Pincoffs (see p018) in the hip southern development zone. If you want to stay central, book into one of the six themed rooms at A Small Hotel (Witte de Withstraat 94, T 414 0303), a charming townhouse in the cultural quarter. The Manhattan Hotel (Weena 686, T 430 2000), formerly The Westin, in WZMH Architects' Millenniumtoren, is a good business option; and the courtyard rooms at the canalside Bilderberg Parkhotel (Westersingel 70, T 436 3611) offer a sense of retreat, while those in Mecanoo's zinc-clad tower enjoy a contemporary edge.

For full addresses and room rates, see Resources.

Hotel New York

The 400-seat restaurant here rather trades off the 1917 Jugendstil ('Nieuwe Kunst') building's landmark status, attracting hordes of visitors and after-work drinkers despite its mediocre fare. The hotel itself is a different matter. Located in the former Holland America Line HQ (see p009), it has 72 high-ceilinged accommodations, each with a unique style. The views from the riverside aspect are almost unsurpassed in Rotterdam, and the Corner and Balcony Rooms have a sense of space that will go to your head. We recommend the Board Room Suite (above) with its superb vistas, wainscoting and original fireplace, or the Tower Room Meuse Side – a crash-pad with a spiral staircase in the middle and a three-quarter-size sea-captain's bed. *Koninginnenhoofd 1, T 439 0500, www.hotelnewyork.nl*

Suitehotel Pincoffs

The divine Pincoffs is the baby of Karen Hamerlynck and her husband Edwin van der Meijde, former journalists who have turned an 1879 custom house into a 17-room boutique hotel, with help from stylist Mirjam van der Rijst. The property blends innovative design with superb service and high-tech pampering. Art Suite XL, by artist Liesbeth van Ginneken, features two bathrooms, one with a steam-room shower, a vast bedroom (opposite) and separate TV room. All of the art and much of the furniture have been produced using recycled materials – we love the rocking chairs (above) upholstered, by Marlene den Dekker, in old Dutch jute mailbags. Pincoffs somehow manages to be both muscularly corporate and slightly camp.
Stieltjesstraat 34, T 297 4500,
www.hotelpincoffs.nl

Mainport

One of Rotterdam's newest additions, the luxury Mainport has views over the city's oldest harbour and the modern towers along the Maas, while being only a stone's throw from arts street Witte de Withstraat. Designed by MAS architects with interiors by Feran Thomassen, the hotel opened in 2013, and its 215 rooms are spread over eight floors, each themed on a continent using colourful motifs; the Antarctic Waterfront Spa Room (right) stands out for its jacuzzi and sauna. For guests who don't have private wellbeing facilities, Spa Heaven on the eighth floor has a Turkish steam room, a hammam and a sauna with panoramic views. The sense of far-flung shores is maintained in the quayside Restaurant Down Under's melting-pot Australian cuisine, which includes Japanese sashimi and Argentinean beef.
Leuvehaven 77, T 217 5757,
www.mainporthotel.com

Stroom

Loosely translated as 'electricity flow',
Stroom is part of the old power station
complex by the Lloyd line docks – the
area known as Lloydkwartier is now a
hive of TV studios and ad agency offices.
Stroom's designer, Robert Winkel, worked
out that the average hotel guest spends
about 70 per cent of their waking time in
the bathroom, which he made the main
feature of the studios. Walk into one of
the duplexes, such as Split Level Studio
15 (above), and a large corner tub and sink
stand where the bedroom would usually
be; other features include a double shower
and a Bose iPod dock. The bed (opposite)
is stowed upstairs. Light enters through
a glass roof and slits in walls, so views are
minimal. However, gadgetry abounds in
the 21 rooms and the four spacious Urban
Lofts each have three flatscreen TVs.
Lloydstraat 1, T 221 4060,
www.stroomrotterdam.nl

24 HOURS

SEE THE BEST OF THE CITY IN JUST ONE DAY

Rotterdam offers architecture and art, cuisine and clubbing, plus, naturally, plenty of water, facilitating Europe's largest container port (see p034) and a striking dockland conversion. The city centre is compact and flat, so ask your hotel for a bicycle; they will be complimentary or available for a small charge. Cycle lanes are extensive, separated from motor vehicles and have their own traffic lights. And with your trusty steel steed between your legs, you can manage breakfast at Dudok (opposite), lunch at Uit Je Eigen Stad (see p044) and a molecular dinner at FG Restaurant (see p037), and still burn calories on your way back home.

For a creative fix, make your way down Witte de Withstraat, past conceptual art haven TENT (see p032) and the contemporary visual culture-led MAMA (No 29-31, T 233 2022) to Museumpark, for paintings by Old Masters such as Bosch, Bruegel and Rembrandt at Museum Boijmans Van Beuningen (see p030). Opposite, Het Nieuwe Instituut (see p076) has amalgamated once-independent establishments for architecture, design and e-culture; a ticket here includes entry to Sonneveld Huis (see p026), to experience the genius of Leendert van der Vlugt and Johannes Brinkman. To view more functionalist delights, visit the Van Nelle Factory (see p066), or ride south to Erasmusbrug (see p010) to admire De Rotterdam (see p012), before crossing to the emerging Katendrecht district. *For full addresses, see Resources.*

09.00 Dudok

Willem Marinus Dudok is best known for the Chicago Prairie School-style town hall and schools he designed in Hilversum, from 1915, but his name is immortalised in Rotterdam's expansive grand café. He conceived it for an insurance firm in the 1940s, installing a 6m-high staffroom, acres of glass and simple columns for decoration. Since 1991, it has been one of the city's premier hangouts, not least because of its famous apple pie, said to be the best in the Netherlands. Dudok also serves its own muffins, cookies, cupcakes and other patisserie, as well as Smit & Dorlas coffee, and has piles of (usually Dutch-language) newspapers. It's buzzy and hectic, but no one hurries to leave, which is not a problem, since it closes at 1am on Fridays and Saturdays.
Meent 88, T 433 3102, www.dudok.nl

10.00 Sonneveld Huis
Formed in 2013, Het Nieuwe Instituut (see p076) displays temporary exhibitions that may or may not enthral, but admission to Sonneveld Huis (part of the institute) is worth the €10 ticket alone. It's a faithful, evocative restoration of a 1933 modernist residence occupied by the family of a Van Nelle Factory (see p066) director, who was a convert to the Dutch functionalist movement, Nieuwe Bouwen. The factory's architects, Brinkman & Van der Vlugt, produced a villa heavily influenced by Le Corbusier, with a steel frame that allowed a strip of window along the facade of the first floor (see p028). The furniture, most of it designed by Willem Hendrik Gispen, and fittings, including an internal phone system and integrated radio speakers, were at the cutting-edge of technology design and have been faithfully replicated.
Jongkindstraat 12, T 440 1200,
www.hetnieuweinstituut.nl

Sonneveld Huis

11.00 Museum Boijmans Van Beuningen

Near Rem Koolhaas' Kunsthal (see p078) is this architecturally less radical but artistically impressive museum. It hosts visiting exhibitions, and has a superb permanent collection of modern and conceptual works, including pieces by Dalí, Beuys, Warhol and Oldenburg, and Studio Wieki Somers' *Merry-Go-Round Coat Rack* (above). But arguably its key exhibits are in its Old Masters collection; it has the best Bruegel and Bosch works in the country, including the former's *Little Tower of Babel*. The 1935 building, designed by Ad van der Steur, includes the Garden Gallery (opposite), and gained an extension with a crisp glass skin from Ghent firm Robbrecht en Daem in 2003. Like most Rotterdam museums, it shuts on Mondays. *Museumpark 18-20, T 441 9400, www.boijmans.nl*

14.30 TENT

Part of Rotterdam's Centrum Beeldende Kunst, TENT is dedicated to identifying trends in the work of locally based and commissioned international artists, who are asked to explore how the city can influence their work. TENT is keen on conceptual and interdisciplinary pieces, such as Han Hoogerbrugge's 'La Grande Fête des Voyeurs' retrospective (right), displaying them in a series of big white rooms in an imposing 19th-century school building. In 2014, the facade and ground floor were renovated, the aim being to make TENT more accessible at street level, and to give co-tenants Witte de With (T 411 0144) – a contemporary art centre – extra exhibition space in the shared building. From here, it's an easy stroll over to Oude Haven for a lunch of modern Dutch cuisine at Mooii (see p051). *Witte de Withstraat 50, T 413 5498, www.tentrotterdam.nl*

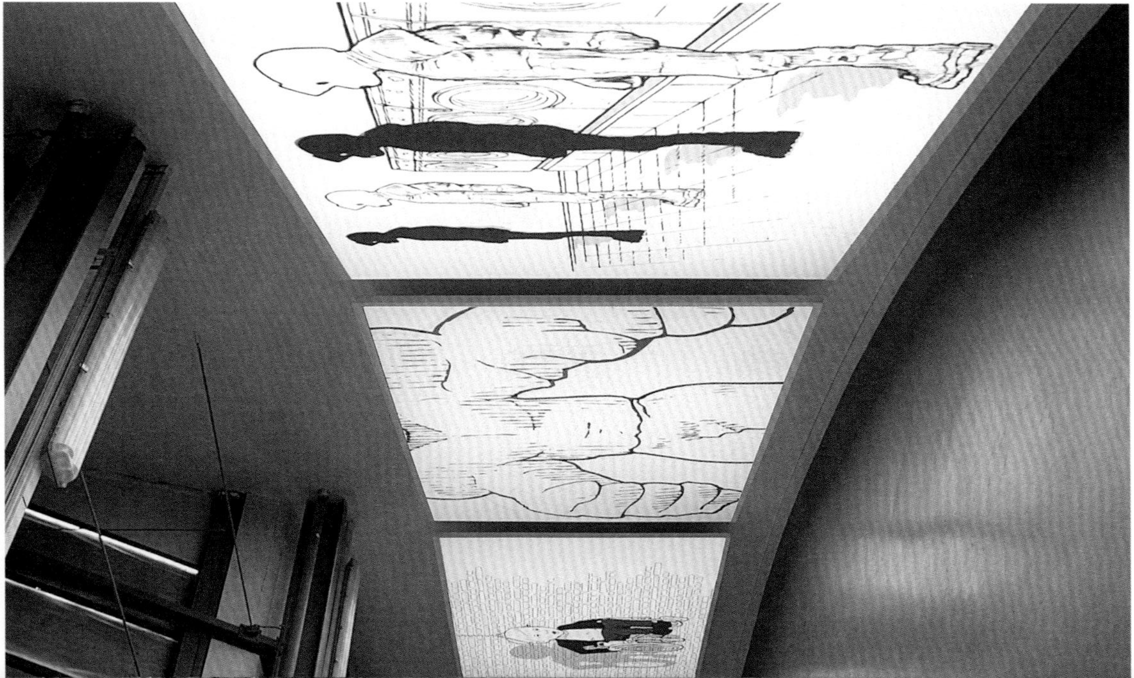

16.30 Boat tour

The 75-minute trip around the docks from Spido's Willemsplein jetty (www.spido.nl), starts beneath Erasmusbrug (see p010) before turning round to head past the periscope-like Shipping and Transport College (pictured), designed by architects Neutelings Riedijk and completed in 2006. Then it's on through forests of cranes and cities of shipping containers. The scale of it all will boggle your landlubbing mind.

19.00 De Witte Aap

'The White Monkey' is a popular venue on Rotterdam's designer drag, one of the few old, tree-lined streets in the city. The tiny interior is dominated by an S-shaped bar and a giant cracked mirror. There's enough room for a few green upholstered booths and stools, but most evenings it quickly becomes standing-room only. The venue's cachet is down to its location and the zippy service, something of a rarity in Holland.

Owner Ron Sterk took over in the late 1990s, when this street was shedding its sketchy reputation. Drinks consist of little more than special beers and spirits, but it's open late, there are DJs on Fridays and Saturdays until 4am, and it attracts a good-looking bunch. The heated terrace is also a coveted spot for a late-afternoon beer. *Witte de Withstraat 78, T 414 9565, www.dewitteaap.nl*

20.30 FG Restaurant

Formerly Restaurant Ivy, FG is helmed by head chef, founder and co-owner François Geurds, who previously worked as Heston Blumenthal's sous chef at The Fat Duck, where he became a convert to molecular gastronomy. His menu features nitrogen-frozen tomato piccalilli, and dishes such as Anjou pigeon, foie gras and cherry sorbet with benzaldehyde – an almond-flavoured organic compound – served in a masculine space, all exposed stone and upholstered booths. During the 11-course tasting menu, some 30 aromas are released to ensure that the diners benefit from a full olfactory experience. Don't think that FG is a mere gimmick, though; Blumenthal came to the opening in February 2009 and Rotterdam has been enchanted ever since.
Lloydstraat 294, T 425 0520,
www.fgrestaurant.nl

23.00 Maassilo
A concrete former grain warehouse that
has parts dating to 1906, this club is a
triumph of post-industrial reclamation.
A 2004 refurb added lifts and flooring,
but left the fabric rough and industrial,
complete with grain hoppers and ducts.
Among its resident nights, one has a
fashion-meets-underground aesthetic;
we like the monthly Factory 10 parties.
Maashaven Zuidzijde 1-2, T 476 2452

URBAN LIFE

CAFÉS, RESTAURANTS, BARS AND NIGHTCLUBS

As in many European cities, the days of Rotterdam's mega-clubs are over, as people embrace more intimate locales in which to do their partying. Currently, such venues are conveniently focused just east of Centraal Station, including the outdoor Biergarten (Schiestraat 18, T 062 470 8305) and the graffitied electronica den Perron (Schiestraat 42, T 062 470 8305), in a former post office. If it must be old-school-style raving, head to erstwhile grain store Maassilo (see p038), which hosts club nights once or twice a week.

The country's big swinging chefs, François Geurds (see p037), Erik van Loo (see p047) and Herman den Blijker (see p052), battle it out at the highest level, but if you're unable to get a table in their restaurants, a new wave of talent, such as Jim de Jong (see p042), offers an equally delectable alternative for half the price and wait. Otherwise, head to Deliplein in Katendrecht for various options, including De Matroos en het Meisje (Delistraat 52, T 215 2764), Vislokaal Kaap (see p050) and quirky Indonesian-inspired café Kopi Soesoe (Sumatraweg 15, T 062 481 6754). There are plenty of places to discover on Witte de Withstraat, which competes with Nieuwe Binnenweg to be the most essential street in the city. The former probably shades it because of its proximity to the cultural delights of Museumpark (see p024) and the chichi shopping, but both offer designer interiors and gritty boozers to suit all moods. *For full addresses, see Resources.*

Oliva

Alex Verburg and Cees van der Burg's light, bright, southern Italian restaurant has been a firm favourite of Rotterdam's chattering classes since it opened in 2001. The lofty ceilings and pale walls, decorated with painted 'pasta curtains' on one side (above), contrast with dark green tiling, contemporary tables and a wooden floor. Oliva presents a new menu every day, based around whichever fine ingredients have been delivered, and incorporates homemade pasta, organic vegetables and ethically treated meat where possible. The kitchen is open, as is Oliva's philosophy – if you order one of the specials, the chef will come out to talk you through the provenance of the ingredients and the region it hails from.
Witte de Withstraat 15a, T 412 1413, www.gustoliva.nl

Restaurant De Jong

Part of the Mini-Mall strip under the old railway arches, which includes Lokaal (see p060), Restaurant De Jong is young chef Jim de Jong's stage. Having interned with the likes of Heston Blumenthal and Gordon Ramsay, he co-launched De Jonge De Jong in Katendrecht, before going solo. Unveiled in 2013, this French-influenced open kitchen offers a choice of two four-course dinners that change weekly and feature a range of rather surprising combinations: tomato juice with smoky olive oil in a soup; or skate on ox-heart cabbage with bottarga and white grapes. The soul and chanson music that fills the simple tiled interior forms a good basis to continue your night at jazz haunt Bird (T 737 1154), a few doors down.
Raampoortstraat 38, T 465 7955, www.restaurantdejong.nl

Uit Je Eigen Stad

'From Your Own City' is an award-winning concept that transformed an abandoned harbourside into a hybrid urban farming initiative, organic local food market and restaurant. Founded by Johan Bosman (concept), Bas de Groot (green fingers) and Huibert de Leede (business), Uit Je Eigen Stad grows its own vegetables, breeds its own fish and raises its own chickens, connecting urbanites with their food sources. The selection of in-house ingredients is supplemented by farmers just outside town, and the changing lunch menu includes dishes like triple-seeded pavé bread with liver sausage, lovage salt and mayonnaise. A little off the beaten track, the venue can be reached via the new Dakpark, a remarkable green strip that covers a shopping street stretching from Hudsonplein to Marconiplein.
Marconistraat 39, T 820 8909,
www.uitjeeigenstad.nl

Picknick

You can indeed get a takeaway picnic from breakfast-and-lunch spot Picknick, but a similar experience can be had by settling down on one of its two patios. Inside, bearded freelancers take advantage of the wi-fi, but the atmosphere remains homely due to a mishmash of wooden tables and chairs contrasting with the raw concrete walls. There are daily organic and locally sourced specials: for breakfast, try a tasting platter with cheese, ham, a soft-boiled egg, juice and a scone with cream; for lunch, the grilled sandwich filled with mushrooms, gorgonzola, shallots and tarragon is hard to beat. Founder Femke Snijders has various other redevelopment projects across the city, including Picknick Aloha Bar, set in a former water park.
Mariniersweg 259, T 280 7297,
www.picknickrotterdam.nl

Parkheuvel

In a circular pavilion at the bottom of what Rotterdammers call 'the park' (it was the first in town), Parkheuvel is the city's best fine-dining restaurant and has great views of the river. Patron Erik van Loo is Dutch culinary royalty and Parkheuvel is the eighth Michelin-starred kitchen he has worked in; this establishment currently has two, plus 18 Gault & Millau points. Van Loo took over in 2006, and the interiors,

designed in a patterned art deco manner, were conceived by his wife, Anja. The cooking is delicate and refined without being overly fussy. The signature dishes include goose liver marinated in pinot gris with beetroot; ravioli of Bresse chicken accompanied by langoustines; and snails with potato purée, walnut and black garlic.
Heuvellaan 21, T 436 0530,
www.parkheuvel.nl

De Pijp
The Dutch word *gezelligheid* describes a cosy and convivial social scene. Which brings us to De Pijp, a restaurant with wooden furniture and a slate floor, which has been serving traditional fare since 1898 and is popular with business folk and politicos. The food, such as wild-boar stew, is hearty, if a little heavy on the port sauces and sautéed potatoes.
Gaffelstraat 90, T 436 6896

Vislokaal Kaap

Katendrecht was once known for randy sailors and the prostitutes paid to love them. Now, connected to Kop van Zuid via a footbridge, the gentrifying district's Deliplein is a culinary hit, attracting Rotterdammers from all over, especially to Thai restaurant Deli Bird (T 485 5288). However, it is relaxed spot Kaap, which specialises in fish, that is the current leader of the pack. Chef Daniël Baris, who has a background in macrobiotic cooking, established his name with the 'stubbornly sustainable' Deli Z&M (T 280 0980). In a similar vein, Kaap's green kitchen is vegetarian-friendly, but it is the simple seafood dishes, such as cod ceviche with grapefruit, and *moules frites*, that keep the regulars coming back.
Delistraat 48, T 423 2222,
www.restaurantkaap.nl

Mooii

Oude Haven, full of rickety wooden boats and circled by waterside bars, has become something of a hotspot for local students (the university is nearby) and tourists. But Mooii caters to a very different market. Its cool lounge/terrace attracts the beautiful people after work, while during the day it is *the* lunch destination for business types and the fashionable shopping set. It was given its palette of grey, white and cream by co-owner Frank Roolaart – who was advised by architect Piet Blom (see p070) – whereas the major twig, branch and foliage statements adorning the place are courtesy of floral stylist Krijn Verboom. Chef Gerard van Gelderen oversees the modern Dutch cooking, which has touches of the Mediterranean and the Orient. *Oost-Wijnstraat 8-16, T 411 2295, www.restaurantmooii.nl*

Las Palmas

Big, bald Herman den Blijker is known as
Holland's equivalent of Gordon Ramsay;
quite literally, as he took up the TV role
when the *Kitchen Nightmares* programme
was sold to Dutch television. Las Palmas
is his flagship venue, a buzzy, Marseille-
style restaurant on the ground floor of
the 1953 former Holland America Line HQ
(see p009), which has a distinctive modern,
curved addition by the Amsterdam-based
architects Benthem Crouwel on its roof.
Set on the redeveloped Wilhelminapier
by the river, Las Palmas was redesigned
in 2010 by den Blijker, who left lots of the
ducting and the concrete columns exposed
in the vast dining room. It is now a great
space and the bouillabaisse alone makes
the journey over the bridge worthwhile.
*Wilhelminakade 330, T 234 5122,
www.restaurantlaspalmas.nl*

De Schouw
Next door to De Witte Aap (see p036),
on Witte de Withstraat, is an altogether
grittier drinking establishment, yet one
where you're likely to find most of the
creatives from Rotterdam's cultural
quarter. The interior has changed little
since it opened in 1940. On one side is
a plain wooden bar with tall red stools,
while on the other are a couple of high-
backed vinyl-upholstered booths. The
smoke-stained walls are covered in old
posters, retro beer ads and other pubby
paraphernalia. A tiny exhibition space
(40cm x 67cm x 115cm) by the front door
is dubbed the 'world's smallest gallery',
and since 2001 it has premiered a new
artist's work every Thursday at 9pm. De
Schouw has a convivial, boho vibe – a dive
bar with a warm, nicotine-tainted heart.
Witte de Withstraat 80, T 412 4253

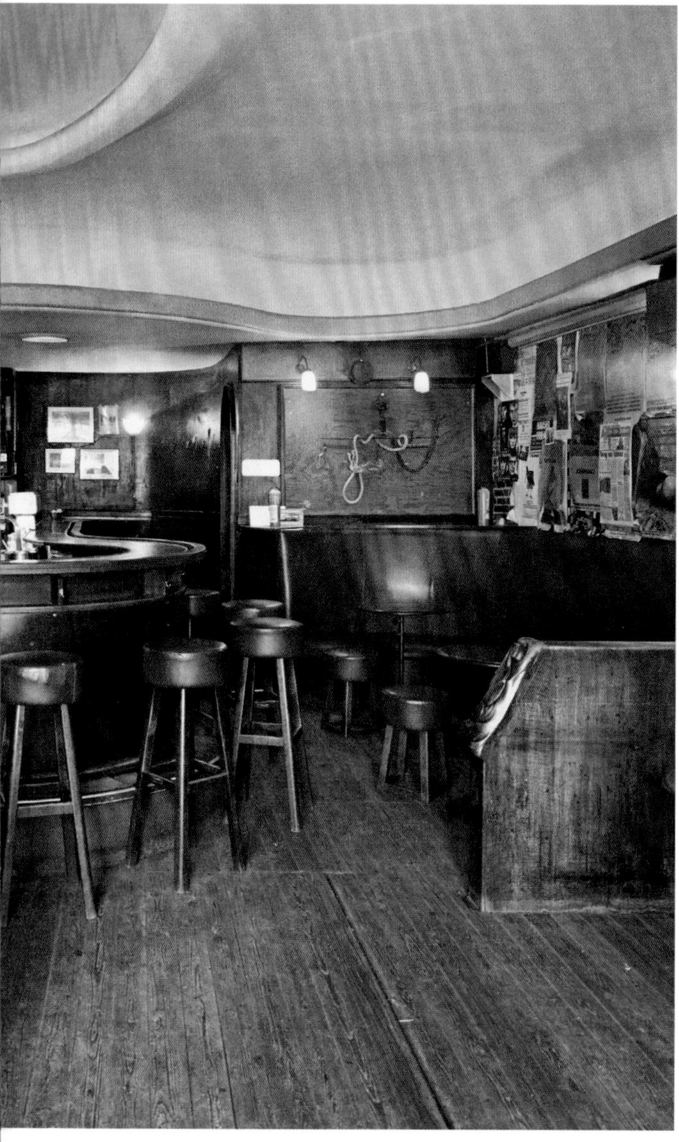

Wijn of Water

It seems only right that Rotterdam, a port city metaphorically built on the shipping container, should have a restaurant made out of them. 'Wine or Water', which is set beside the Shipping and Transport College (see p034), is fashioned out of nine 12m corrugated containers, painted turquoise, one of which is upended to create a tower, while others have glass walls. A delightful, unpretentious structure, designed by

Caroline Bijvoet and opened in 2005, Wijn of Water is perfectly suited to both its maritime environment and the unfinished district in which it's located. The sheltered terrace is a great place for a beer in the sunshine. The cuisine is French, Asian and Italian, and there's a daily menu of specials alongside a quarterly à la carte.
Loods Celebes 101, T 478 3006,
www.wijnofwater.nl

Lux

Due to its contemporary design, Lux, which opened in the early 1980s, was a draw for the city's new-wave crowd. As they grew up, it continued to host the wonky end of the chattering classes; Rem Koolhaas is still a regular. It had a slick makeover by architect Chiel van der Stelt in the 1980s, and in 2013 it was revamped again when chef-owner Milan Gataric took the helm. Today, it's considerably smaller and much more intimate, although many original elements remain and there's an outside seating area if it gets too tight. The food is top-flight regional Italian, and the menu bursts with sophisticated dishes such as stewed octopus with tomato, red wine and basil, and homemade sausage with white beans and lardo.
'S-Gravendijkwal 133, T 476 2206, www.restaurantlux.nl

Euromast Brasserie
Tear yourself away from the views to appreciate Dutch designer Jan des Bouvrie's retro-chic 2004 refurb of the restaurant in the Euromast (see p009), featuring Verner Panton 'S' chairs, as well as those by des Bouvrie himself (pictured). Chef Robert Seidenburg produces excellent international fare.
Parkhaven 20, T 436 4811,
www.euromast.nl

Lokaal Espresso

Launched in 2011, coffee bar Lokaal is
one of a handful of hip venues in Central
District East's Mini-Mall, accessible via
the remarkable Luchtsingel, a wooden
bridge that connects the city centre
to this former station in once-forgotten
Rotterdam North. On-trend neighbours
include Restaurant De Jong (see p042),
comic-book store Comiquest (T 061 698
7490), and a variety of fashion pop-ups.
Designed by local firm Weaponofchoice,
the space is thoroughly minimal, with
pine, brass and glass creating a canteen-
like atmosphere. Using a good selection
of beans from Latin America, and a La
Marzocco espresso machine, Lokaal is
a solid alternative to the proliferation of
coffee chains that not even this city has
managed to escape. When it's sunny, the
terrace here is a perfect spot for a brew.
Raampoortstraat 34b, T 466 6665,
www.lokaal-espresso.nl

INSIDER'S GUIDE

ZELDA BEAUCHAMPET, DESIGNER

Founder of Dutch jewellery and accessories label The Boyscouts (www.theboyscouts.nl), Zelda Beauchampet's style is urban yet organic, and grounded in the local; very much like her favourite haunts in Rotterdam. She recommends taking the water taxi to Katendrecht to explore Deliplein (see p050), before making the short walk to Damage Playground (see p085). 'It's a concept store for all those who appreciate fashion and style,' she says. Serving bruschetta made with fresh sourdough bread, Urban Espressobar (Nieuwe Binnenweg 263, T 477 0188) is Beauchampet's favourite lunch spot; afterwards, she will swing by Opperclaes (Claes de Vrieselaan 103; Thursday to Saturday, 12pm to 5pm), 'a gallery for up-and-coming artists, curated by those who share their passion for graphic design, photography and street art'.

In the city centre, Dearhunter (Eendrachtsweg 55a, T 270 9742) provides a vintage fix, whereas Margreeth Olsthoorn (see p081) 'feels like a gallery and catwalk at the same time'. Around Central Station, she adores the locally designed products at Groos (see p082), describing the store as 'the face of what's hip in Rotterdam'. Nearby, Biergarten (see p040) is 'a summer oasis for beer lovers', although for cocktails she recommends Twentysix (Kruiskade 26) where 'the atmosphere is never flat, and the owner often replaces his chef to serve his favourite food to regular customers'.

For full addresses, see Resources.

ARCHITOUR
A GUIDE TO ROTTERDAM'S ICONIC BUILDINGS

Even before the Luftwaffe gave Rotterdam's architects a blank canvas, the city had secured a reputation for modernist design. Le Corbusier described Johannes Brinkman and Leendert van der Vlugt's Van Nelle Factory (see p066) as 'outstanding', while one of the very few buildings to be replicated after WWII was Jacobus Johannes Pieter Oud's 1925 De Stijl De Unie (Mauritsweg 34-35, T 433 5833), rebuilt on a new site in 1986 with a facade by Carel Weeber (see p075). Largely, though, postwar Rotterdam focused on masterplanning a new city by developing social housing and realising ideas like Lijnbaan, the first pedestrian shopping street.

Twenty-first century Rotterdam is still a magnet for innovative contemporary architects and designers looking to set up base, such as OMA (see p078) and MVRDV, and it's also a welcoming playpen for adventurous projects. Kop van Zuid and Lloydkwartier gave scope to vertiginous feats of engineering – the cantilevered plane is as ubiquitous as a hedgerow in the English countryside. The frenzy continues with ambitious schemes such as De Rotterdam (see p012), the Centraal Station revamp (see p074) and organic initiatives like Luchtsingel bridge (www.luchtsingel.org), meant to symbolically reconnect Rotterdam North with the rest of the city. Serious architecture fans should take a tour – try Rotterdam Archiguides (T 433 2231, www.rotterdam-archiguides.nl).

For full addresses, see Resources.

The Red Apple

Former OMA partner Kees Christiaanse, now of architects KCAP, not only designed The Red Apple, where interiors are by Jan des Bouvrie, he laid down the masterplan for the redevelopment of the entire island of Wijnhaven. The building, completed in 2009, takes its name from the colour of its anodised aluminium panels as well as the fact that apples used to be exported from this section of the docks. There are three volumes – the 120m-high tower and the truncated triangular block are filled up with 231 apartments, while the lower part houses retail space, offices, restaurants and cafés. The residences at the top of the triangular edifice share a dramatic internal patio that cuts a hole through the centre of the building. As always in Rotterdam, there is also a big, precipitous overhang.
Wijnbrugstraat

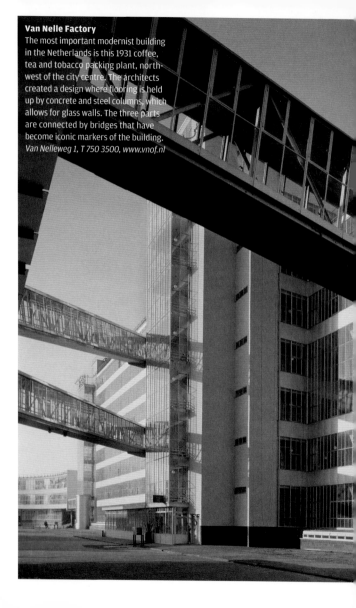

Van Nelle Factory
The most important modernist building
in the Netherlands is this 1931 coffee,
tea and tobacco packing plant, north-
west of the city centre. The architects
created a design where flooring is held
up by concrete and steel columns, which
allows for glass walls. The three parts
are connected by bridges that have
become iconic markers of the building.
Van Nelleweg 1, T 750 3500, www.vnof.nl

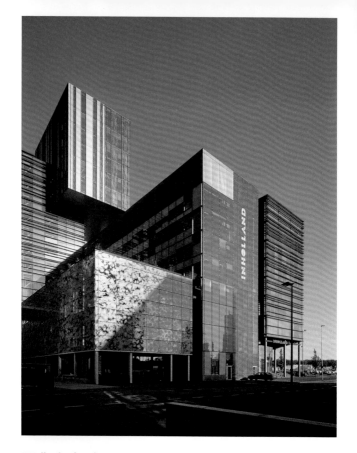

INHolland University

Erick van Egeraat's 2001 design for the science university campus produced a slender glass rectangle featuring a curved lower facade on pilotis, with louvred glass above. Internally, an attractive atrium surrounded by glass-walled rooms gave rather more drama to the building than the exterior. Egeraat's extension, opened in 2009, added some of the showboating elements that Rotterdammers demand from their architects. A nine-storey bridge, from which a partly cantilevered tower emerges, rests on a new low-level volume, which connects the existing structure to a hall of residence at the rear. Coherence is maintained through yellow prints etched on to some of the glass facades, while the bridge uses louvres to relate to the original construction. And very nice it is too.
Posthumalaan 90

De Hef

The Lift (De Hef), as Koningshavenbrug is known locally, has a special place in the hearts of Rotterdammers. When it opened in 1927, it was hailed as a piece of landmark modernist technology. Civil engineer Pieter Joosting used concrete counterweights to lift its middle section up two 60m towers. The bridge has since inspired avant-garde filmmakers, poets and architects. Something about its exposed engineering appeals to the locals' image of themselves as serious grafters, especially when compared with dainty Amsterdammers. It ceased to be operational in 1993, when a railway tunnel was built under the river and De Hef was scheduled for demolition. It was saved by a protest movement and is now a national monument, its middle section permanently raised to allow shipping to pass.

Cube Houses

Architect Piet Blom was inspired by the medieval bridges that housed shops and homes when he designed the pedestrian bridge and Cube Houses that cross Blaak. The 51 cubes, completed in 1984, have been described as 'treehouses', with their lower point fixed in a hexagonal post. You enter through the concrete 'trunk' and go upstairs, passing the only vertical walls, into the cube itself, which has a kitchen/ living room on the first floor, bedrooms above and a room in the apex (opposite). The project is much photographed and there is an open house, but it was not a major success. The apexes are often too hot to occupy, space is lost to the sloping walls, and few people use the bridge as it's quicker to cross the highway below. *Overblaak 70, T 414 2285, www.kubuswoning.nl*

The Bridge

Utrecht architects JHK's 2005 Unilever
HQ would look good stood up straight.
But perched 25m in the air on steel stilts
and lying on its side, it's a treat, due to
its streamlined aesthetics, the futuristic
vision of its urban planning and the
flamboyant engineering – the 133m
frame was assembled downriver and
rolled into place over the factory below.
Nassaukade 5, T 439 4308

Centraal Station

Rotterdam is growing as a national and international transport hub. In 2007, Centraal Station had 110,000 daily users; it's projected to have 320,000 by 2025. Three celebrated firms, West 8, Benthem Crouwel and Meyer en Van Schooten had a hand in its revamp, completed in spring 2014. Under a swooping metallic roof, the glass-and-timber concourse is open and well lit; the walkway has been expanded to six times its original width; and a bicycle tunnel runs underneath the station to Rotterdam North. Two granite sculptures, the *Speculaasjes*, from the former station, are placed above the tunnel entrance. Locals have dubbed the terminal 'Station Kapsalon', a nod to the dish of chips, cheese and kebab meat that is served in a container as shiny as the roof.
Stationsplein 1

De Peperklip

Viewed from above, this building is shaped like (you guessed it) a paperclip. At the time of its construction in the late 1970s (it was completed in 1982), architect Carel Weeber maintained that frumpy Dutch design was being used to disguise the paltry budgets for many social housing schemes. He argued that prefabrication could provide better and bigger homes. Not, however, prettier ones, at least from the outside. One for the architectural purists, De Peperklip's pre-cast concrete exterior is faced with six colours of tile, which ensure that the 555 apartments are externally indistinguishable from one another. The rounded ends are between seven and nine storeys high and in places are too close together, creating narrow alleys with sound and wind issues.

Rosestraat, www.peperklip.nl

Het Nieuwe Instituut

It's as if this building is trying to display as many ideas on the outside as inside. Jo Coenen was the winner of a contest to design this establishment, opened in 1993 as the Netherlands Architecture Institute (NAi), which merged with two other cultural organisations to create Het Nieuwe Instituut (see p026) in 2013. A banana-shaped concrete volume on piers houses the archives; a rectangular brick box surrounds the three exhibition spaces; and, in-between, a glass and steel block for the offices and study hall appears suspended between columns, hanging from an overshooting pergola (pictured). The everything-but-the-kitchen-sink approach works, thanks to the rarefied context of Museumpark. *Museumpark 25, T 440 1200, www.hetnieuweinstituut.nl*

Kunsthal

Rem Koolhaas has several projects in the pipeline for his hometown, even after finishing De Rotterdam (see p012). But the best way to engage with OMA's famed architect is still the Kunsthal. Opened in 1992, it has a series of ramps intersected by a path. On one side is an auditorium, with a ramp floor doubling as the roof of the restaurant below. On the other side, the exhibition spaces are of contrasting volumes: the basement has steel columns dressed as tree trunks; a side gallery above features a vertigo-inducing steel-grating floor; and the main space's huge window overlooks the road. Travertine and black glass abuts concrete, corrugated plastic and galvanised metal grilles. Exhibitions are advertised on the tower on the roof. *Westzeedijk 341, T 440 0301, www.kunsthal.nl*

SHOPPING

THE BEST RETAIL THERAPY AND WHAT TO BUY

We've left out some of Rotterdam's biggest fashion names to focus on its less well-known offerings, many of which are located in City Centre and Museumpark. Included are retail experiences unique to the city, from the offbeat designs of local creatives sold at mini-emporium Groos (see p082) to menswear store/gallery/record shop Damage Playground (see p085). Stylish knitwear by young designers, put together by elderly volunteers at Granny's Finest (Karel Doormanstraat 320, T 870 0233), is a distinct example of the typically idiosyncratic Dutch approach to fashion. Of course, prominent labels have not been completely overlooked; there is Margreeth Olsthoorn's progressive fashion boutique (opposite) and, nearby, the lingerie at Marlies Dekkers (Witte de Withstraat 2, T 280 9184), which is highly covetable and also available globally.

The finest department store in the city, Marcel Breuer's 1957 De Bijenkorf (Coolsingel 105, T 800 0818), is a concrete cube faced with hexagonal panels (the name means 'beehive'). More major brands are found on Lijnbaan and Binnenwegplein, but we advise heading east of here, to the Maagd van Holland Kwartier, to view the fun Dutch design at Depot Rotterdam (Pannekoekstraat 66a, T 414 4448), and Christian Ouwens (Oppert 2, T 243 0043; open Thursday to Saturday), which stocks contemporary art, books and design from the likes of Piet Hein Eek, Droog and Hella Jongerius. *For full addresses, see Resources.*

Margreeth Olsthoorn

In her new digs, which brings together the concepts of now-defunct boutiques MGHO and MGH2O, designer and stylist Margreeth Olsthoorn continues her calling as a local champion of avant-garde fashion, showing a tightly curated selection of labels for men and women. The rawness of the space, all exposed concrete and mobile fixtures and mirrors, is a perfect complement to the stock, which leans heavily on dark tones, asymmetric cuts and scarcely embellished fabric. Dutch and Belgian names feature strongly, ranging from Raf Simons and Maison Martin Margiela to Rotterdam's own Jeroen van Tuyl and jewellery from The Boyscouts (see p062). Launched in 2013, Olsthoorn's emporium also hosts fashion shows, art exhibits and pop-ups. *Schilderstraat 5, T 282 7542, www.margreetholsthoorn.nl*

Groos

In up-and-coming Central District East, not far from Centraal Station (see p074), the charming Groos combines design, fashion, books, food and music, all conceived and/ or made in Rotterdam. The owners Tjeerd Hendriks and Joost Prins know just how to wire visitors into the city; Groos is named after the Dutch word for 'pride'. Browse the colourful geometric prints by graphic designer, artist and DJ Nicole Martens,

experimental electronica releases from Clone Records, and David Derksen's Dewar Light (above), €845, all of which can be taken home in a vibrant New Shoppingbag by Susan Bijl. Groos is set in Schieblock (www.schieblock.com), a building filled with creative entrepreneurs, where you can grab a beer or a snack and catch a DJ.
Schiekade 203, T 414 5816, www.groosrotterdam.nl

ANSH46

Wouter Leenders and Kelly Erentreich's upscale mens- and womenswear boutique, 'Another Shop 46', moved here in 2013 from its former home on Mauritsweg. Spacious and modern, the new interior is now as luxe as the stock. A plush suede-upholstered seating area and slick copper counter creates a comfortable setting in which to browse the rails of garments, marked by simple lines, muted palettes and high-tech materials. The figure '46' is the dialling code for Sweden, and ANSH46 offers the ultimate minimalist label from Scandinavia, Acne, alongside brands that can be a little harder to find in Rotterdam, including Alexander Wang, 3.1 Phillip Lim and Carven. Perfume by Diptyque and Dries Van Noten round out the selection. *Van Oldenbarneveltstraat 99, T 233 9182, www.ansh46.com*

Damage Playground

When this bricks-and-mortar concept store and gallery opened in Katendrecht in 2012, Damage was already established as a webshop. Co-owners and brothers Alexandre and Anibal Furtado collate art, books, magazines, furnishings and music that appeals to a sophisticated hipster clientele. However, the focus remains on the menswear, which runs the gamut from United Nude shoes to pieces from vegan designers Good Guys Don't Wear Leather. Damage has recently started to retail women's clothes, including threads from Rotterdam-based label Nieuwe Meuk. Using this playground as a home and base, the brothers now hope to set up more projects in the surrounding area, which was once the poorest in the Netherlands.
Hillelaan 29, T 751 1587,
www.damageclothing.com

Galerie VIVID

Having relocated to The Red Apple (see p065) in 2010, VIVID's Saskia Copper and Aad Krol continue to do as they've done for decades: showcasing and selling the best in contemporary Dutch design and conceptual art by hosting a number of exhibitions a year. Whatever VIVID may be displaying, be it furniture, ceramics or the witty yet wholly useable products and household objects for which the Dutch are renowned, it's worth a browse. Hella Jongerius, Richard Hutten, Jurgen Bey and local studio Minale-Maeda (first solo exhibition, left) are among those to have been represented here. The gallery has also travelled overseas, most recently to design fairs in Basel and Miami, and, in 2014, VIVID celebrated its 15 year anniversary with an exhibition at the Kunsthal (see p078). Closed Mondays.
Scheepmakershaven 17, T 413 6321, www.galerievivid.com

SPORTS AND SPAS

WORK OUT, CHILL OUT OR JUST WATCH

These are torrid times for football-mad Rotterdammers, whose beloved Feyenoord (see p094) last tasted European glory with a UEFA Cup win in 2002. Even at home, the 28-year dominance of Holland's big three – Feyenoord, Ajax and PSV – was broken when unfashionable AZ Alkmaar won the league in 2009, soon followed by FC Twente. Still, the locals love to talk football, even as their hearts break at all the Dutch coaches and players working abroad.

Sailing is popular too, thanks to the city's aquatic surroundings and its own small lake, the Kralingse Plas, where former Olympian Henk van Gent has a sailing centre (Plaszoom 350, T 412 1098). From April to December, boats can be hired by the hour, from a little Escape dinghy to a Tirion with 26 sq m of sail, or lessons can be booked, usually for two or three hours. There are also beaches if you fancy some sun and a dip. The best spa option is the Elysium Centre for Wellbeing (Kooilaan 1, Bleiswijk, T 524 1166), located some 30 minutes from the city centre, which offers Dead Sea mud treatments, reflexology and Thai and shiatsu massages. The huge complex comprises 23 saunas, steam baths, indoor and outdoor pools, an ornate domed and tiled hammam and extensive gardens.

Runners do their thing in Het Park and across the Erasmusbrug (see p010), but your best option for exercise is also your best option for transportation – a bike borrowed from your hotel.

For full addresses, see Resources.

New Fire Tower, Outdoorpark Reusel

Just over an hour south of Rotterdam, not far from the Belgian border, is a splendid woodland facility that, as in so much of the Netherlands, is fun and ingenious. The centrepiece is a 26m tower that acts as an observation deck and anchor point for sporty activities. The contemporary design – six timber-sided cubes – is by Maud van Banning of local firm Ateliereen and fits perfectly into its environment.

The exterior of the lower two cubes is used as a 15m climbing wall, and the tower is the starting place for various aerial rope walkways and obstacle courses that lead off into the woods. You can also abseil down from the top or get on the zip line that reaches speeds of 100kmh. Climbing slots can be reserved on the website. *Burgemeester Willekenslaan, Reusel, T 06 5726 8206, www.outdoorparkreusel.nl*

Pilates Rotterdam
This very serious studio is run by former dancers Javier Velazquez and Mariska Barnard, who studied with none other than Joseph Pilates' protégée Romana Kryzanowska. The light, lofty space is fully equipped with all the requisite machinery (some of which resemble instruments of torture). Sessions here cater for both individuals and groups.
Rijnhoutplein 2, T 276 3511

Schorem

Combining 1920s aesthetics with a 1950s
rock'n'roll attitude, this new but decidedly
old-school barbershop launched in 2011.
Proprietors and tattoo-loving pals Leen
and Bertus use traditional techniques for
their varied selection of haircuts, which
includes pompadours, crew cuts, and
fades. Stressing the genuine boys' club
credentials, Schorem's staff also impart
in-depth expert advice on waxing those
moustaches, sculpting your sideburns
and trimming manly beards – all offered
with a whisky on the side. It's a full-on and
often hilarious experience that is worked
out to the tiniest retro detail. There are
no appointments, just walk-ins, so it's also
the perfect place to go for a trim before
an evening out on the nightlife strip it's
located on. And if it isn't already crystal
clear: no women are allowed.
Nieuwe Binnenweg 113, T 241 0309,
www.schorembarbier.nl

Stadion Feyenoord
Named after the port-workers' district
to the south, Feyenoord's motto is 'Not
words, but deeds'. It's a neat summary
of the city itself. The club's stadium is
nicknamed De Kuip ('The Tub') because
of its curving two-deck stands. Originally
completed in 1937, it was renovated and
given hospitality facilities and a roof in
1994. You can buy match tickets online.
Van Zandvlietplein 1, T 492 9444

ESCAPES

WHERE TO GO IF YOU WANT TO LEAVE TOWN

In this packed-out corner of Europe, with its super-efficient rail links, a two-hour journey from Rotterdam could put you not only in several other cities, but a couple of different countries. The most obvious escape is Amsterdam, just 50km down the road but a world away in spirit and aesthetic. We would overnight in the Marcel Wanders-designed Andaz (Prinsengracht 587, T 020 523 1234) or the glam Conservatorium (Van Baerlestraat 27, T 020 570 0000). Also consider the equally historic but much more sedate Maastricht, home to two excellent hotels, the Kruisherenhotel (Kruiserengang 19-23, T 043 329 2020) and Derlon (Onze Lieve Vrouweplein 6, T 043 321 6770), and Eindhoven (opposite), whose design palaces and creative sensibilities are only 80km away.

So close you could cycle there is Delft (see p102), a Golden Age gem made rich by the Dutch East India Company, immortalised by the artist Vermeer and renowned for its blue-and-white pottery. A trip to The Hague (see p098) should be combined with the seaside town of Scheveningen, not for its amusement arcades, but for the superb Beelden aan Zee museum and sculpture park (see p100). A quieter stretch of coast in the western Netherlands is the watery wonderland of Zeeland. The best place to dine in this province is the slightly chintzy but two-Michelin-starred Manoir Restaurant Inter Scaldes (Zandweg 2, Kruiningen, T 011 338 1753).

For full addresses, see Resources.

Van Abbemuseum, Eindhoven

It might be the Philips company town, but Eindhoven has turned an industrial history built on lightbulbs into a specialism in science, research, high-tech innovation and design nous that echoes through its many cultural outlets. Not least of which is the Van Abbemuseum contemporary art gallery, where a muscular 2003 extension (above) by Abel Cahen created space to display more works by Picasso, Kandinsky and Mondrian, alongside a core collection of early 20th-century Dutch modernists. Other highlights in Eindhoven include its 'school of cool', the Design Academy (T 040 239 3939), which produced Jurgen Bey and Hella Jongerius among others. Visit the website (www.designacademy.nl) for details of all the upcoming shows. *Bilderdijklaan 10, T 040 238 1000, www.vanabbemuseum.nl*

The Hague

You can take a day trip to The Hague from Rotterdam (it's only 25km), but then you'd miss the chance to stay at Hotel Des Indes (T 070 361 2345), one of the country's finest lodges since 1881. A 2005 refurb by Parisian Jacques Garcia blended its venerable features with swish modern amenities, as found in the Executive Room (above) and the bar (opposite). From here, head to Scheveningen, a kiss-me-quick beach resort to the north-west of the city. Buried in the sand dunes is architect Wim Quist's splendid Museum Beelden aan Zee (T 070 358 5857). It launched as a private institute, but now receives lottery funds to acquire international works and to exhibit retrospectives of artists like sculptor Fritz Wotruba (overleaf). Tom Otterness' 'Fairy Tale Sculptures by the Sea' is a permanent installation of 23 bronzes on the boulevard.

Museum Beelden aan Zee, Scheveningen

UOT Library, Delft
Delft trades on its car-free centre, leafy canals, tin-glazed pottery and Vermeer's grave. But this 1998 library, designed by architects Mecanoo for the University of Technology, is our draw. A grassy slope, used as a park in summer, is pierced by a cone with a base forming study areas inside the wedge-shaped building. Some 80,000 titles are available to the public.
Prometheusplein 1, T 015 278 5678

NOTES
SKETCHES AND MEMOS

RESOURCES

CITY GUIDE DIRECTORY

A

ANSH46 084
Van Oldenbarneveltstraat 99
T 233 9182
www.ansh46.com

B

Biergaarten 040
Schiestraat 18
T 062 470 8305
www.oktoberfestrotterdam.com

De Bijenkorf 080
Coolsingel 105
T 800 0818
www.debijenkorf.nl

Bird 043
Raampoortstraat 26
T 737 1154
www.bird-rotterdam.nl

The Bridge 072
Nassaukade 5
T 439 4308

C

Centraal Station 074
Stationsplein 1

Christian Ouwens 080
Oppert 2
T 243 0043
www.christianouwens.nl

Comiquest 060
Katshoek 35
T 061 698 7490
www.comiquest.nl

Cube Houses 070
Overblaak 70
T 414 2285
www.kubuswoning.nl

D

Damage Playground 085
Hillelaan 29
T 751 1587
www.damageclothing.com

Dearhunter 062
Eendrachtsweg 55a
T 270 9742

Deli Bird 050
Delistraat 46
T 485 5288

Deli Z&M 050
Veerhaven 13
T 280 0980
www.zenmdelicatessen.nl

Depot Rotterdam 080
Pannekoekstraat 66a
T 414 4448
www.depotrotterdam.nl

Design Academy 097
Emmasingel 14
Eindhoven
T 040 239 3939
www.designacademy.nl

Dudok 025
Meent 88
T 433 3102
www.dudok.nl

E

Elysium Centre for Wellbeing 088
Kooilaan 1
Bleiswijk
T 524 1166
www.elysium.nl

Euromast Brasserie 058
Euromast
Parkhaven 20
T 436 4811
www.euromast.nl

HOTELS

ADDRESSES AND ROOM RATES

A Small Hotel 016
Room rates:
double, from €140
Witte de Withstraat 94
T 414 0303
www.asmallhotel.nl

Andaz 096
Room rates:
double, from €350
Prinsengracht 587
Amsterdam
T 020 523 1234
www.andaz.hyatt.com

Bilderberg Parkhotel 016
Room rates:
double, from €145
Westersingel 70
T 436 3611
www.bilderbergparkhotel.nl

Conservatorium 096
Room rates:
double, from €325
Van Baerlestraat 27
Amsterdam
T 020 570 0000
www.conservatoriumhotel.com

Derlon Hotel 096
Room rates:
double, from €150
Onze Lieve Vrouweplein 6
Maastricht
T 043 321 6770
www.derlon.com

Hotel Des Indes 098
Room rates:
double, from €145;
Executive Room, from €205
Lange Voorhout 54-56
The Hague
T 070 361 2345
www.hoteldesindesthehague.com

Kruisherenhotel 096
Room rates:
double, from €400
Kruisherengang 19-23
Maastricht
T 043 329 2020
www.designhotels.com/kruisheren

Mainport 020
Room rates:
double, from €150;
Antarctic Waterfront Spa
Room, from €230
Leuvehaven 77
T 217 5757
www.mainporthotel.com

The Manhattan Hotel 016
Room rates:
double, €100
Millenniumtoren
Weena 686
T 430 2000
www.manhattanhotelrotterdam.com

Hotel New York 017
Room rates:
double, from €100;
Corner Room, €180;
Tower Room Meuse Side, from €195;
Balcony Room, €215;
Board Room Suite, from €250
Koninginnenhoofd 1
T 439 0500
www.hotelnewyork.nl

nHow 016
  Room rates:
  double, €150
  Wilhelminakade 137
  T 206 7600
  www.nhow-hotels.com
SS Rotterdam 016
  Room rates:
  double, from €40
  3e Katendrechtsehoofd 25
  T 297 3090
  www.ssrotterdam.nl
Stroom 022
  Room rates:
  double, from €85;
  Split Level Studio 15, from €125;
  Urban Loft, from €175
  Lloydstraat 1
  T 221 4060
  www.stroomrotterdam.nl
Suitehotel Pincoffs 018
  Room rates:
  double, from €130;
  Art Suite XL, from €245
  Stieltjesstraat 34
  T 297 4500
  www.hotelpincoffs.nl

WALLPAPER* CITY GUIDES

Executive Editor
Rachael Moloney

Editor
Ella Marshall
Authors
Steve Korver
Paul McCann

Art Editor
Eriko Shimazaki
Designer
Mayumi Hashimoto
Map Illustrator
Russell Bell

Photography Editor
Elisa Merlo
**Assistant Photography
Editor**
Nabil Butt

Chief Sub-Editor
Nick Mee
Sub-Editor
Farah Shafiq

Editorial Assistants
Rodrigo Márquez
Emilee Jane Tombs

Interns
Harriet Ball
Maurício Mendes

**Wallpaper* Group
Editor-in-Chief**
Tony Chambers
Publishing Director
Gord Ray
Managing Editor
Oliver Adamson

Original Design
Loran Stosskopf

Contributor
Kim Heinen

Wallpaper* ® is a
registered trademark
of IPC Media Limited

First published 2010
Revised and updated
2014

All prices are correct at
the time of going to press,
but are subject to change.

Printed in China

PHAIDON

Phaidon Press Limited
Regent's Wharf
All Saints Street
London N1 9PA

Phaidon Press Inc
65 Bleecker Street
New York, NY 10012

Phaidon® is a registered
trademark of Phaidon
Press Limited

www.phaidon.com

A CIP Catalogue record for
this book is available from
the British Library.

ISBN 978 0 7148 6839 4

PHOTOGRAPHERS

Maayke de Ridder
Rotterdam city view,
inside front cover
De Rotterdam, p012
Hotel New York, p017
Suitehotel Pincoffs,
p018, p019
Mainport, pp020-021
Museum Boijmans Van
Beuningen, p030, p031
Restaurant De Jong,
p042, p043
Uit Je Eigen
Stad, pp044-045
Picknick, p046
Vislokaal Kaap, p050
Las Palmas, pp052-053
Lux, p057
Lokaal Espresso,
pp060-061
Centraal Station, p074
Margreeth Olsthoorn, p081
Groos, p082
ANSH46, p084
Damage Playground, p085
Galerie VIVID, pp086-087
Schorem, pp092-093

Misha de Ridder
Van Nelle Factory,
pp066-067

Erik & Petra Hesmerg
Museum Beelden
aan Zee, pp100-101

Job Janssen
TENT, pp032-033

Antje Quiram
Erasmusbrug, pp010-011
Witte Huis, p013
Schouwburgplein,
pp014-015
Stroom, p023
Dudok, p025
Sonneveld Huis,
pp026-027, pp028-029
Shipping and Transport
College, pp034-035
De Witte Aap, p036
FG Restaurant, p037
Maassilo, pp038-039
Oliva, p041
Parkheuvel, p047
De Pijp, pp048-049
Mooii, p051
De Schouw, pp054-055
Wijn of Water, p056
Euromast Brasserie,
pp058-059
The Red Apple, p065
INHolland University, p068
De Hef, p069
Cube Houses, p070, p071
The Bridge, pp072-073
De Peperklip, p075
Het Nieuwe Instituut,
pp076-077

Kunsthal, pp078-079
Pilates Rotterdam,
pp090-091
Stadion Feyenoord,
pp094-095

Christian Richters
University of Technology
Library, pp102-103

Nadine Stijns
Zelda Beauchampet, p063

ROTTERDAM
A COLOUR-CODED GUIDE TO THE HOT 'HOODS

MUSEUMPARK
Hop between Rotterdam's myriad cultural highlights in OMA's superbly designed park

LLOYDKWARTIER
Cool industrial conversions dominate this recently formed quarter on the river's edge

OUDE WESTEN
Buzzy bars and the city's most interesting shops line the best streets in this gritty area

WATERFRONT/NOORDEREILAND
Head to the island in the Maas for its villagey vibe, and to Waterfront for its lively scene

SCHEEPVAARTKWARTIER
Hang out with the city's smart set in the bars and restaurants of this attractive district

CITY CENTRE
Venues to the north draw fashionable clubbers; the centre is full of major-label shops

DELFSHAVEN
This affluent area made for ambling is as close to Amsterdam as you'll get in this town

KOP VAN ZUID
High-design high-rises have reshaped the skyline in the south bank's regeneration zone

For a full description of each neighbourhood, see the Introduction.
Featured venues are colour-coded, according to the district in which they are located.